The Home 1939-1945

A Guide for Family Historians

Stuart A. Raymond

THE FAMILY HISTORY PARTNERSHIP

Published by
The Family History Partnership
57 Bury New Road
Ramsbottom, Bury
Lancahire BL0 0BZ

in association with
S.A. & M.J. Raymond
38 Princess Gardens
Trowbridge
Wiltshire BA14 7PT

Webpage: www.stuartraymond.co.uk
Email: samjraymond@btopenworld.com

First published 2012

ISBN: 978 1 906280 37 6

Printed and bound by
Berforts Information Press
Southfield Road, Eynsham
Oxford OX29 4JB

Contents

Acknowledgements

My thanks to the members of the Family History Partnership, who urged me to write this book, and especially to Richard Ratcliffe, who checked my first draft, and to Bob Boyd, who saw the book through the press. Apart from my own photographs, the illustrations are mostly taken from Wikimedia.

1. Introduction

The aim of this book is to help you trace who did what on the Home Front during the war, and to research the history of your family in the war years. The country was mobilised for total war, so there were few who failed to make their contribution. Much attention has been devoted to tracing members of the armed forces, but they were not the only people who contributed to the war effort. Many others also had their part to play – policemen, firemen, farmers, civil servants, railwaymen, ARP personnel, the Home Guard, indeed, virtually everyone who stayed at home. Their contribution deserves to be recognised.

There are a variety of general sources of information available to researchers, for example, the civil registers, national registration, electoral registers. These will be described below. One of the major problems in researching World War II ancestors is the huge range of more specialist material available. There were few central government departments which were not required to extend their functions and activities to support the war effort; indeed, war needs led to the creation of a number of new departments, for example, the Ministry of Home Security. This activity is reflected in the holdings of The National Archives (TNA). The same applied to the activities of local government. Every local council, for example, had to create Emergency Air Raid Precautions Committees (usually abbreviated to ARP, and later called Civil Defence Committees), to deal with the effects of bombing. All played a role in the evacuation of children from the major cities. These and other activities created a mountain of paper records.

The archives of institutions and businesses also reflect war-time activities. They continued to employ staff, and personnel files may be available to help you trace the working lives of your families. They sometimes undertook fire-watching, ran Home Guard units, evacuated their activities to safer areas, or were bombed out, with resultant paper work which may also be of interest. The ARP records of the Westminster Bank, for example, can now be found amongst the archives of the Royal Bank of Scotland **http://heritagearchives.rbs.com/ wiki/Westminster_ Bank_Ltd,_London,_1836-1969.** The Palace of Westminster had its own fire-fighting brigade. Here, security was an extra consideration, as the firemen needed access to all parts of the Palace; the Parliamentary Archives **www.parliament.uk/archives** holds a file giving the names of ARP firemen vetted by Scotland Yard in 1942-4.

Many archives are still to be adequately catalogued and indexed. Unfortunately, the catalogues which are available do not always make it clear whether files on particular topics contain information likely to be of use to family historians. Pot luck may be the order of the day. Nevertheless, much useful information is available on record office online catalogues. Record office websites are listed at Archon **www.nationalarchives.gov.uk/archon**. Many record office catalogues are also available on the union catalogue at A2A: Access to Archives **www.nationalarchives.gov.ukj/a2a.** Both of these should be checked. Although A2A is sometimes duplicated in record offices' own online catalogues, it may have additional information. On the other hand, many record office catalogues include information which is not on A2A.

Archiveshub **http://archiveshub.ac.uk** should also be checked. This is the union catalogue for the archives held by universities and colleges. It includes, for example, the holdings of Warwick University's Modern Records Centre **www2.warwick.ac.uk/services/ library/mrc**, which holds many business, institutional, and trade union records.

Another important union catalogue is provided by Aim25 **www.aim25.ac.uk**. This covers archives held by higher education institutions, learned societies, cultural organisations, etc., in the London region.

Much information is also available in TNA, and can be identified by browsing through its catalogue **www.nationalarchives.gov.uk/records**. If you want to undertake a general search, try the new 'Discovery' catalogue, preferably using the 'advanced search' mechanism. If, however, you already know the TNA class you wish to search, press the button headed 'catalogue', and enter the class number. You can browse through individual piece numbers in a particular class by calling up the first piece in that class, and pressing the 'browse from here' button.

Many personal accounts of war-time life have been published, in both print and online. Evacuees, civil servants, Home Guard officers and men, ARP wardens – all have written accounts of their experiences. Some of these accounts have been published, and are available in libraries. Much unpublished material has been deposited in record offices. No less than 47,000 accounts collected by the BBC are online at:

♦ WW2 People's War: an archive of World War Two Memories: written by the people, gathered by the BBC
    www.bbc.co.uk/history/ww2peopleswar.

Mass Observation **www.massobs.org.uk** was established immediately before the war, and took as its remit the task of recording memories. It recruited some 500 participants who recorded their experiences in diaries. It also undertook a variety of local social surveys. Unfortunately, few names can be identified in these diaries and surveys, but they do enable you to picture the setting in which your ancestors lived their lives. An introduction to the Mass Observation Archive at the University of Sussex is provided by Dorothy Sheridan's *The Tom Harrison Mass-Observation Archive: a guide for researchers* (University of Sussex Library, 1991).

Numerous projects to record war-time memories have been conducted by a variety of different organisations. The results of these projects can be found in many libraries and museums, as well as on the internet. The Recollections of WWII website **www.recollectionsofwwii.co.uk** provides a useful listing of national, local, and internet collections of sound recordings.

It is important to note that some of the records mentioned here may be closed to public consultation until after a lengthy time lapse – perhaps seventy or a hundred years. Record office catalogues usually provide details of such restrictions. Recent Freedom of Information legislation has, however, opened up many of these records, and you may be permitted to view them. Bear in mind that catalogues may not have been updated to take this legislation into account. If you locate details of apparently closed records you would like to view, check to make sure whether such restrictions still apply.

It must be emphasised that this book is a work in progress – as, indeed, is the cataloguing of archives dating from this period. More sources are likely to be unearthed in the next few years. It is quite likely that the serious researcher will discover sources not mentioned here. If you do so, please let me know.

It must also be emphasised that there are innumerable books on the war. Those mentioned here are rarely the only ones that deal adequately with their subjects; it would be impossible in a book of this length to cite all the texts that are worth consulting.

2. The Civil Registers and Other Death Records

If you are searching for particular individuals, the civil registers of births marriages and deaths are the first sources to check. They are vital sources for all family historians. The registers themselves cannot be consulted directly; instead, it is necessary to purchase certificates of births, marriages and deaths from either the General Register Office, or from district registrars.

The information provided by full certificates (do not be tempted to buy 'short' certificates, as they give no information of value to the family historian) is as follows:

Birth certificates

When and where born
Name if any
Sex
Name and surname of father
Name, surname, and maiden surname of mother
Occupation of father
Signature, description and residence of informer
Name entered after registration

Marriage Certificates

Place of marriage
When married
Names and surnames of the parties
Ages
Condition (i.e. marital status)
Rank or profession (if any)
Residence at the time of marriage
Father's name and surname
Rank or profession of father
Whether by banns, licence, or registrar's certificate
Signatures of parties, minister or registrar, and witnesses

Death Certificates

When and where died
Name and surname
Sex
Age
Occupation
Cause of death
Signature, description, and residence of informant
When registered
Signature of registrar

In order to obtain certificates, indexes must be searched. There are a number of ways in which this can be done. The General Register Office (G.R.O.) indexes are available free at FreeBMD **www.freebmd.org.uk**, although the birth indexes for the war years are not yet complete. Full indexes are available on a number of commercial sites, such as Ancestry **www.ancestry.co.uk** and Find My Past **www.findmypast.co.uk**. Many libraries and record offices hold the indexes on microfiche. It is also possible to ask the G.R.O. to undertake a search for you.

The indexes provide you with the information needed to order a certificate from the G.R.O., i.e. the full name, the year of registration, together with the volume and page number of the register. Certificates can be ordered via the G.R.O. website **www.gro.gov.uk/gro/content/certificates/faqs-birth-death-marr.asp**.

Certificates can also be issued by district registrars. The G.R.O. indexes cannot be used to obtain these; district registrars have their own separate indexes. Some of these are freely available online; for a gateway, visit UKBMD **www.ukbmd.org.uk**.

The civil registers are not the only source of information on civilian war casualties. 67,000 civilians killed during the war are commemorated on the Civilian Roll of Honour, which is now incorporated in the Commonwealth War Graves Commission's Debt of Honour database **www.cwgc.org/debt_of_honour.asp**. Mortuaries sometimes compiled lists of the victims of bombing raids. It may be worth searching for such lists amongst local authority records. For example, Uckfield's 'Record of civilian deaths due to war operations: register compiled from mortuary returns', covering 1940-44, is held by East Sussex Record Office (DW/B/69/1). Police records may also help. Metropolitan Police registers of casualties are now in TNA, class MEPO4/306-11. There is also a register of murders and deaths by violence in London, now in TNA, MEPO20. Such registers sometimes give much more detail than can be found in the civil registers.

Sudden and suspicious deaths (except those caused by bombing) were subject to coroners' inquests. Consequently, the records of coroners may include useful information. The Coroner kept a register of the cases he dealt with. This will give dates, names, ages, sex, and details of the coroner's findings. Registers and other coronial records that have been deposited in local record offices are listed in:

♦ GIBSON, JEREMY, & ROGERS, COLIN. *Coroners' Records in England and Wales.* 3rd ed. Family History Partnership, 2009.

Some records may still be held by coroners themselves. Unfortunately, many have been destroyed. However, inquests were frequently reported in newspapers, which should perhaps be checked first (see chapter 7 below).

A variety of other registers of births, marriages, and deaths are also available. There is, for example, a register of prison burials in TNA class HO324. Parish registers are particularly important, especially given the fact that civil marriage registers were copied from duplicates of parish marriage registers. Birth, marriage, and death announcements in newspapers may also be useful. For more detailed guidance on sources for these vital events, consult:

- RAYMOND, STUART A. *Birth and baptism records for family historians*. Family History Partnership, 2010.
- RAYMOND, STUART A. *Marriage records for family historians*. Family History Partnership, 2010.
- RAYMOND, STUART A. *Death and burial records for family historians*. Family History Partnership, 2011.

3. National Registration

Returns from the census taken in 1931 were destroyed during the war. The census due in 1941 had to be cancelled. Consequently, census information for the war years and the preceding period is rarely available. However, for family historians, the records of national registration offer a partial substitute. The demands of war made it necessary to compile a register of the entire population. Mobilisation and mass evacuation were thought likely to create many problems. Information was needed in order to implement manpower planning and perhaps rationing.

Registration was implemented by the Registrar General, in much the same way as the census. National registration day was 29th September 1939. 65,000 enumerators distributed and collected registration forms, and issued identity cards at the same time. The card had two pages; at the top of each page, the enumerator entered the individual's name and identity card number. The latter consisted of a four-letter area identity code, plus the line number of the enumerator's schedule, for example, AAAA 12/3 would indicate area AAAA, schedule 12, the 3rd person in the household. A space was also left for the individual's address, and his signature, but initially this was to be left blank, 'until further notice'.

Approximately 46,000,000 buff-coloured cards were issued. In December 1939 it became possible to obtain an ID card with space for a photograph. These green cards were available for those who needed special provision to prove their identities. The following year, instructions were issued to fill in addresses and sign the cards, which from then on had to be carried at all times (under 16s were exempt from this requirement). In 1943, on the introduction of rationing, both buff and green cards were replaced with a blue card for adults, and a buff card for children. The original cards for children were not replaced at this time. Identity cards were abolished in February 1952, but the identity numbers used formed the basis for National Insurance numbers. These are still in use.

Identity cards can occasionally be found amongst family papers, although most have been lost. The registration information, however, has been kept. This information includes name, sex, date of birth, marital status, occupation, and whether in the armed forces or reserves. These details were used as the basis for the National Health Service central register when it was formed in 1948, and which lists everyone registered with a General Practitioner. Until recently, no access to this database was allowed. However, Freedom of Information legislation has led to limited availability of the records. Data related to individuals who have died can now be released, for a substantial fee. Information can be requested on a named individual, on up to nine co-residents, on a specific address, and on up to ten residents at that address. This only applies to the original 1939 register, and not to later additions to the register. It is important to note that individuals were recorded where they were on registration night. If they were in the services, in hospital or prison, travelling, or anywhere else, they will not be recorded at their home address.

For details of this service, visit:

♦ NHS Information Centre: 1939 Register Service
   www.ic.nhs.uk/services/1939-register-service

For an overview, visit:

♦ The 1939 National Identity Card
   www.1911census.org.uk/1939.htm

4. Electoral Registers

If the National Register was fully accessible, it would offer the most comprehensive list of the war-time population available. Its limited availability means that the researcher seeking a comprehensive listing must be satisfied with the electoral registers. By the beginning of the war, all adults aged 21 and over (apart from Peers, convicts, lunatics, and aliens), were entitled to register to vote. That does not, of course, mean that everyone did register; there was undoubtedly under-registration. Perhaps more seriously, the exigencies of war-time meant that, although registers were normally compiled annually, the 1939 register had to serve until the next one was compiled in 1945. The 1939 register listed everyone who was eligible to vote on 1st June 1939, and who registered; it came into force on 15th October 1939. The fact that the next register was not compiled until 1945 means that this source cannot be used to trace the massive dislocation caused by evacuation, bombing, and the exigencies of war. Nor can it be used to identify servicemen in the way that the absent voters registers of World War I could be used.

Despite these caveats, the electoral registers of 1939 and 1945 provide baselines from which it is possible to trace the movements of individuals, and to reveal the names of all adults who lived in particular households. They are arranged by constituency, ward, and street. Unfortunately, there are no indexes.

Electoral registers are usually held by local record offices and/or local studies libraries. A major collection is also held by the British Library. A full listing of surviving registers is provided by:

♦ GIBSON, JEREMY. *Electoral registers 1832-1948; and burgess rolls: a directory to holdings in Great Britain.* 4th ed. Family History Partnership, 2008.

For a very detailed listing of the British Library's holdings (which includes a useful introduction), consult:

♦ CHEFFINS, R.H.A. *Parliamentary constituencies and their registers since 1832.* British Library, 1998.

The Birmingham registers of 1939 and 1945 are available online at:
www.midlandshistoricaldata.org

5. Taxation Records

Where they are available, the records of taxation can be valuable sources of information. They can locate members of your family in time and place. For the war period, the most comprehensive listings are provided by rating records, although land tax records may also be useful.

Rates provided a major source of income for local authorities. They were levied on either householders or landowners. Rate books contain lists of those liable to pay, with assessments of the value of their property, and the amount that they were required to pay. Valuation books record the value of properties. They may also record the names of occupiers and/or owners, but not necessarily so. Both types of record are arranged by ward or parish, and then by street. They are rarely indexed, and have been little used by genealogists. A comparison of rate lists and electoral registers may provide useful information.

The land tax was imposed by central government; its origins go back to 1692. Returns were made annually, and include the names of proprietors, occupiers, and sums assessed. It was, however, possible to redeem the land tax in return for commutation payemnt. By 1939, a large proportion of payments had been commuted, and consequently many fewer names appear in the records than can be found in returns for earlier centuries. Nevertheless, it is still worth checking this source.
Survival of land tax returns for this period is very patchy. Those returns which are available can be found in local record offices, and are fully listed by Jeremy Gibson, et al, in their *Land and window tax assessments* (2nd ed. Federation of Family History Societies, 2004).

6. Trade Directories

For this period, trade directories are one of the most useful and easily available sources available to genealogists. The golden age of directory publishing was the period immediately prior to the outbreak of war. War presented problems to directory publishers. The paper required was scarce, and the manpower to conduct the research needed was difficult to find. Consequently, the number of directories published declined. In many cases, directories that had previously been regularly issued ceased publication in 1939 or 1940. This applied particularly to the large county and regional directories issued by firms such as Kelly & Co. Town directories had more staying power: for example, there were two war-time editions of *Kelly's directory of Newark and neighbourhood,* in 1940 and 1942.

The primary purpose of directories was to enable tradesmen to identify potential customers, and to find their addresses. They were used for similar purposes by clergymen, magistrates, and other officials. They only include information that was relevant for these purposes. Directories tend to include the names of public officials such as postmasters and clergymen, professionals, and tradesmen. Sometimes they also include residents, but the poorer residents – especially the transients – are not likely to rate a mention. It might be added that compilation was a tedious and time-consuming process. If corners could be cut, especially in war-time conditions, they probably were. Consequently, accuracy may sometimes leave much to be desired.

Despite these caveats, trade directories do provide basic information concerning names, addresses, and occupations. They can be use to check for particular names, to identify the occupiers of a particular property, to trace the location of particular surnames, and to compare with other sources such as rate books and electoral registers.

There are good collections of local directories in most local studies libraries and record offices. Many are available on CD. For this period, few are online, although it is worth checking if you are searching a particular location. A full listing of published directories is provided by:

◆ SHAW, GARETH, & TIPPER, ALISON. *British directories: a bibliography and guide to directories published in England and Wales (1850-1950) and Scotland (1773-1950).* Leicester University Press, 1988.

7. Newspapers

Newspapers are particularly valuable sources of information, but do come with a health warning. There is no good reason why you should believe reports in historic newspapers any more than you would believe their modern-day counterparts. There were stringent controls on the war-time press, especially where top secret information was concerned. Many significant events – for example, the preparations for the D-Day landings – went completely unreported at the time. The government was also concerned that the reporting of disasters would damage morale.

Despite these reservations, newspapers do contain much valuable information for both local and family historians. Attention has already been drawn to their birth, marriage, and death announcements. Awards for gallantry and other medals are frequently mentioned. The tribunals before which conscientious objectors had to appear are likely to be reported in the local press. The Women's Land Army also attracted some press attention.

It is worth searching both local and national newspapers for information. Searching used to be a tedious business, but digitisation is currently making it easy to find masses of information from newspapers online. The first major newspaper to be digitised was *The Times*. Personal subscriptions to the database **http://gdc.gale.com/products/the-times-digital-archive-1785-1985** are expensive; however, it is possible to gain free access through the websites of many public libraries.

The British Library has the largest collection of newspapers in the UK. Over 52,000 periodicals are listed in the catalogue of its Newspaper Library at Colindale. It is currently undertaking a major programme of digitisation. At the time of writing, over 2,000,000 pages from 49 different titles can be viewed online. By the time you read this, many more may be available. The library's catalogue, and its database of digitised images, can be accessed from:

♦ British Library: Newspaper Collections: a guide to our resources
   www.bl.uk/welcome/.html

Many newspapers are also held by local studies libraries and/or record offices. They are frequently available on microfilm; indeed, the Newsplan project arranged the microfilming of numerous local newspapers, in order to ensure their preservation. For details of the Newsplan project, with links to the regional websites where the microfilmed newspapers are listed and located, visit:

♦ British Library: Help for Researchers: Newsplan
   www.bl.uk/reshelp/bldept/news/newsplan/newsplan.html

8. The Home Guard

The amateur military tradition, as I.W. F. Beckett (*The amateur military tradition, 1558-1945.* Manchester, 1991) calls it, was still strong in the Second World War. The Home Guard, Auxiliary Units, the Royal Observer Corps, and ARP (air raid precaution) wardens all played important roles in the defence of Britain.

Home Guard training.

The Home Guard (originally known as Local Defence Volunteers) was founded when Anthony Eden broadcast a request for volunteers. The response was enormous: by the end of June 1940, no less than 1,456,000 men had answered the call. Perhaps half of them had served in the armed forces during the First World War. They were called upon to release the regular army from the duties involved in civil defence, such as garrison duties, anti-aircraft defences, and bomb disposal. By 1943, there were 111,917 enrolled in the Home Guard's Anti-Aircraft units. Another 7,000 were engaged in bomb disposal work, and another 7000 were manning coastal batteries. A total of 1,206 men lost their lives whilst on Home Guard duty.

The Home Guard should not be confused with the Auxiliary Units. Although members of these units wore the Home Guard uniform, they were an entirely separate body. They were raised in the summer of 1940 in order to wage guerilla war if England should be invaded. The uniform was provided in order to blend in,

Home Guard inspection.

and to avoid attracting attention. The British Resistance Organization has a museum **www.parhamairfieldmuseum.co.uk/brohome.html** which is the focal point for research on the Auxiliaries.

Women were not initially recruited to the Home Guard; however, by March 1944 there were 28,000 in the Womens' Auxiliary. These should not be confused with the Womens Territorial Service, which was the womens' branch of the regular army.

Before Eden's call to arms, there had been no preparation. A telegram had been sent to chief constables immediately before the broadcast, warning them that they would have to enrol volunteers, but many police stations were completely unaware that they were about to be deluged with recruits when the first ones arrived. Consequently, the paper work left much to be desired.

There is no comprehensive publicly available list of the men who served, although officers can be identified in the *Home Guard lists* for 1941-44. These are similar in format to the better known *Army lists* (see **www.nationalarchives. gov.uk/records/research-guides/british-army-lists.htm**). Dates of commissions and appointments are given, together with indications of regimental and territorial army postings. Runs can be found in TNA's library, and in other major research libraries.

Home Guard personal records and enrolment forms are available, but only to those who served, or to next of kin. Contact the Army Personnel Centre, Historic Disclosures, Mailpoint 400, Kentigern House, 65 Brown Street, Glasgow, G2 8EX **www.army.mod.uk/welfare-support/23212.aspx**.

Some members of the Home Guard can be traced through the records of the medals they won. Recommendations for the award of the British Empire Medal to Home Guard members is in a file in TNA, class AIR 2/9040. Members of the Home Guard were eligible for the award of the Distinguished Service Order (DSO), normally reserved for the armed forces. The registers of this award are in TNA, class WO390. Other civilian awards that may have been made to members of the force are considered in chapter 12. For a detailed account of the various awards issued to members of the Home Guard, see:

♦ SAINSBURY, J.D. *Hazardous work: an account of the decorations and commendations awarded to members of the* Home Guard *in recognition of acts of gallantry performed on duty 1940-1944.* Welwyn: Hart Books, 1985.

The records of particular units of the Home Guard have sometimes been deposited in both local and national record offices. Amongst the papers of the Metropolitan Police in TNA, for example, are the report books, platoon roll, and miscellaneous correspondence relating to the Roehampton Battalion (MEPO11/101-4). A variety of nominal rolls for Lancashire Home Guard battalions are deposited in the Lancashire Record Office (HG1-13). Somerset Archives & Record Service holds various records relating to the Taunton Battallion (DD\X\POC).

Many histories of Home Guard units have been written, sometimes including lists of those who served. Some units also maintained unofficial war diaries. A number of these histories and diaries are available in TNA, class WO199, and are listed by both Spencer and Mackenzie (see below). Mackenzie also lists titles in the British Library.

Other titles may be found in local studies libraries and record offices. It may also be worth contacting local regimental museums.

A variety of general policy and administrative papers of the Home Guard are held by TNA. Its general registered papers are in WO32 code 66. Operational records are included with papers of the Prime Minister's Office in PREM3. Official Home Guard war diaries are in WO166. These provide daily records of events, reports on operations and exercises, intelligence summaries, etc., written by unit commanders.

For details of other sources held by TNA, see chapter 9 of:
♦ SPENCER, WILLIAM. *Records of the Militia & Volunteer Forces, 1757-1945.* Public Record Office readers guide **3**. PRO Publications, 1997.

The best account of the Home Guard is:
♦ MACKENZIE, S.P. *The Home Guard: a military and political history.* Oxford University Press, 1995.

For a briefer popular account, see:
♦ CARROLL, DAVID. *Dad's army: the Home Guard 1940-1944.* Sutton Publishing, 2002.

9. The Royal Observer Corps

The Royal Observer Corps was established, in association with the RAF, to track and identify enemy aircraft. The great majority of its members were civilian volunteers working in their spare time. They obtained the epithet 'Royal' in recognition of the value of their work during the Battle of Britain.

A list of Corps members, particularly focusing on the war years, is currently being compiled by the Museum of the Royal Observer Corps Museum. The Museum also holds an extensive archive, currently administered by Hampshire Record Office. For details, visit::
♦ Royal Observer Corps Museum
   www.therocmuseum.org.uk/index.html

An overview of the history of the Corps is provided by Wikipedia:
♦ Wikipedia: Royal Observer Corps
   http://en.wikipedia.org/wiki/Royal_Observer_Corps#Second_World_War

For a more detailed account, see:
♦ WOOD, DEREK. *Attack Warning Red: the Royal Observer Corps and the defence of Britain, 1925 to 1975.* 2nd ed. Carmichael & Sweet, 1992.

10. Civil Defence

Civil defence was organized regionally and locally; it was heavily dependant on volunteers. At the height of the war, there were 1,500,000 people involved. It was mainly concerned with coping with the effects of bombing, although preparations were made to deal with an invasion. A brief overview of these preparations is provided by Bernard Lowry's *British home defence 1940-45* (Osprey, 2004).

Amongst other preparations, a war book was compiled for every parish. This detailed strategic information, in accordance with guidance issued by the Ministry of Home Security. A variety of individuals were listed, for example, owners of telephones and cars, members of the Home Guard, first aiders, and those who could undertake heavy work. In order to compile this information a census had to be taken first. Many of these documents have been lost, but a number of war books can be found by searching A2A **www.nationalarchives. gov.uk/a2a**; it is possible that some include copies of the census. These sources are more fully described in Colin Cohen's article on 'The 1942 Barford census and war books: a unique record' (*Local historian* **36**(2), 2006, p.121-7). If they can be found, they may provide valuable information.

ARP wardens were at the heart of the organization of civil defence. They were local people, possessing a detailed knowledge of their area, often working from their own premises. They patrolled the streets making sure that the blackout was observed; they dealt with the immediate aftermath of bombing; they were, at least at the commencement of the war, in charge of public shelters. They were part-time volunteers, trained in fire-fighting and first aid.

In addition to ARP wardens, Civil Defence also required rescue and stretcher parties, control centre staff, and messenger boys. They worked closely with the police, fire service, medical services, and the Women's Voluntary Service.

As far as is known, there is no national register of volunteers; information about those who served must be sought in local rather than national archives. As civil defence was a local responsibility, much can be found amongst the records of local authorities. Wiltshire Archives Service, for example, has lists of Civil Defence personnel in Salisbury (G23/225/2) and Calne (G18/225/11), as well as a wide variety of administrative documents from these and other places. Westminster Archives Centre has a register of part-time ARP staff (CD83), including enrolment forms with names, addresses, and next of kin. Hackney Archives has an extensive series of Civil Defence war diaries recording damage from bombing – and sometimes including photographs. The Imperial War Museum **www.iwm.org.uk** has many civil defence records deposited by ARP personnel who had retained them in their own custody. Voluntary organisations were also involved in ARP work: amongst the records of the Exmouth Branch of the Red Cross in Devon Record Office is a list of its Air Raid Precautions Reserve (6761G/2/20), which includes members' names and addresses, their rank, certificates and qualifications, their date of enrolment, attendances at meetings and their date of discharge.

For a useful brief introduction to civil defence activities, with a number of eye witness accounts, visit:

◆ Fact File: Air Raid Precautions April 1938 – 1945
   **www.bbc.co.uk/history/ww2peopleswar/timeline/factfiles/nonflash/
   a6651425.shtml**

11. War Damage

Damage caused by bombing was extensive, expensive, and serious. Consequently, it led to the creation of many records. These are not prime sources for family historians, but are nevertheless likely to be of interest if ancestors' properties were destroyed. At the least, they will tell you when an ancestor moved house! Those who suffered losses were entitled to claim compensation from the War Damage Commission, whose records are in TNA. AST1 includes claims to compensation. IR36 and IR37 provide details of buildings. Appeals against assessments are in LT1, with an index in LT2. There is a useful listing of other TNA classes covering 'Civil Defence and War Damage During World War 2' at:

◆ Civil Defence and War Damage During World War 2
   **http://yourarchives.nationalarchives.gov.uk/index.php?title=Civil_
   Defence_and_War_Damage_During_World_War_2**

The government needed to have an overall view of the pattern of German bombing, and of the damage caused by raids. ARP wardens, the police, and military personnel, were required to compile reports on every bomb that fell. The forms used recorded when the bomb fell, its type and size, and whether it

A bombed London street.

exploded. A brief description of the damage caused was provided, together with information on air raid warnings and casualty statistics. These reports may be accompanied by sketch maps, and are in TNA, class HO198.

Sometimes, more detailed investigations were undertaken, and recorded in air raid damage files in HO192. These may include plans of buildings and photographs, together with more technical information There are also bomb damage maps – mainly, but not exclusively, for the London Civil Defence Region – in HO193. The data on which all of these reports and maps were based may survive amongst the records of local authorities; there are, for example, many bomb damage maps in London Metropolitan Archives. For fuller details of bomb damage records, consult TNA's research guide:

♦ Bomb Census Survey 1940-1945
  www.nationalarchives.gov.uk/records/research-guides/maps-bomb-census-survey.htm

In the aftermath of bombing, families who had lost their homes had to be re-housed. Local authorities took responsibility for establishing rest centres

A Canterbury street in 1940.

where they could stay until alternative accommodation could be found. Some people stayed in these centres for considerable periods. Rehousing was difficult, as it took time to replace damaged and destroyed housing. Furthermore, billets were free; if they moved out, residents would have to start paying rent again. Many local record offices hold papers relating to these rest centres; these may include details of staffing, and perhaps give the names of inmates. London County Council's rest centres are documented in the London Metropolitan Archives (LCC/WE/RC). These files include admission and discharge registers, as well as log books and details of staffing.

Those who suffered personal injuries were entitled to war disability pensions. Pensions Appeal Tribunals settled disputes about entitlement. Registers of the cases it heard, giving applicants names and the results of the hearing, are in TNA, class BF1. Post-war case files are in BF2, and can be searched by name on TNA's catalogue.

The effects of war on business could also be damaging, and perhaps result in bankruptcy. Notices about bankruptcy proceedings were posted in the *London Gazette*, which can be searched online at **www.london-gazette.co.uk**. There may

Life in the tube.

Growing food
in a bomb crater.

also be notices in the *Times*, and in other newspapers (see above, pp. 14-15). Registers of petitions are in TNA, class B11; many case files (searchable by name in TNA's catalogue) are in B9. A variety of other records are available in TNA; for details, see its leaflet on 'Bankrupts and insolvent debtors: further research' **www.nationalarchives.gov.uk/records/research-guides/bankrupts-insolvent-1710-1869.htm**.

12. Medals

A variety of civilian medals were issued during and after World War II. These included medals for specific occupations, such as firemen and policemen (see below, chapter 18 for these). All such awards had to be gazetted, that is, published in the *London Gazette,* before they could take effect. Many were mentioned in *The Times* and other newspapers. Awards can be searched for by name on the *London Gazette* website, **www.london-gazette.co.uk**. Click on 'Historians – search the Archive', and 'choose a historic event', selecting 'World War II'.

More information may be available in TNA. Recommendations for awards, and other papers relating to them, should be searched. Responsibility for awards was shared by a number of different departments, including, for example, the Home Office, and the Treasury. There are consequently a variety of classes where information can be found; for full details, see the further reading listed below.

Many awards for meritorious service were (and are) awarded in the New Year and Birthday Honours lists. These occasions were sometimes also used to make awards for gallantry. Full lists of awards are given in the London Gazette – usually in the issue for the last day of the year, and for an issue in June. Newspapers also frequently provided full listings. Many files relating to these and other awards can be found amongst the papers of the Prime Minister's Office, and especially in PREM2/100-119.

Files relating to medals won by members of civil defence organizations are in HO207. These frequently relate to awards made in the New Year and Birthday Honours lists, and especially to awards of the British Empire Medal, the George Medal, and the King's Commendation for Brave Conduct. Each file contains recommendations for a particular Civil Defence region.

The minutes and recommendations of the Inter-Departmental Committee for Civil Defence Gallantry Awards are in HO250. These papers are arranged chronologically, so you will need a date to find the recommendation of a specific award.

Unfortunately, there is no index. Some information may also be available in HO207. The records in HO250 are duplicated, at least in part, in records created by the Treasury's Ceremonial Branch (T336). These are arranged chronologicaly, by the date on which they were gazetted.

Some recommendations for civilian gallantry awards can be found amongst Air Ministry records. Although AIR2 is primarily concerned with awards for RAF personnel, recommendations of the Civilian Gallantry Awards committee (an inter-services committee) are in AIR2/8911-4, 8916-8, 8922-3, 9258 and 9264. These include recommendations from all the armed services. Again, these are arranged in rough chronological order.

Admiralty records in TNA also include files relating to civilian gallantry awards. In particular, ADM1/11242 is a file on awards made to Chatham Dockyard workers after the bombing of the dockyards in December 1940.

The King's Medal for Service in the Cause of Freedom, and the Kings Medal for Courage in the Cause of Freedom, were both instituted on 23 August 1945. The first recognized civilian foreign nationals who had helped the Allied cause during World War II, and was awarded 2,539 times; the second was for those who had actively helped British servicemen escaping from enemy territory, at risk of their lives. Records are in TNA, class T 339.

Further information on medals research is provided in TNA's research guide:
♦ Medals: Civilian Gallantry
   www.nationalarchives.gov.uk/records/research-guides/medals-civilian-gallantry.htm

For a much more detailed treatment, consult:
♦ SPENCER, WILLIAM. *Medals: the researcher's companion.* National Archives, 2008.

13. Law and Order

Many records relating to the maintainance of law and order during wartime are available. Crimes were initially recorded in police records, some of which may be found in local record offices. Those relating to the Metropolitan Police are in TNA, as the Met was under the direct control of the Home Office. Personnel records of the police are dealt with below, pp.50-53. Suspects were prosecuted before Justices of the Peace, sitting in Petty and Quarter Sessions; their records can usually be found in local record offices. More serious cases went to the Assizes, and to the central courts; for their records it is necessary to visit TNA. Proceedings in many criminal cases were reported in local and national newspapers (see chapter 7).

Police records have generally not been well looked after, but are nevertheless worth seeking out. Some may be in specialist repositories; for example, the Devon and Cornwall Police Heritage and Learning Resource **www.police heritagecentre.co.uk/index.html** has recently been established. See also the British Police Online Museum **www.pmcc-club.co.uk/museum/index.php**

Crimes entered the historical record in the 'record of crimes committed' book, kept in every police station. This included the name and address of the person making the report, details of the crime, the value of any goods stolen, whether recovered, and whether offenders were apprehended and successfully prosecuted. This is complemented by the 'general report book', also kept in each police station. This is the record kept by investigating officers, and provides details of how crimes were investigated. When a suspect was charged, details were entered in a 'charge register'. These may include descriptions of the persons charged, with their occupation, and details of the court hearing, including the verdict. Each police station also keeps an 'occurrence book', which gives a daily account of work at a police station. These include details of arrests, accidents of all kinds, missing persons, property lost and found, the daily cell inspections, and other occurences. Some of these records have been deposited in local record offices; others may still be with police forces, or in police museums.

Major crimes were prosecuted by the Director of Public Prosecutions. TNA holds his registers of cases prosecuted in DPP3, and some case files in DPP2.

Minor crimes were generally prosecuted at Petty Sessions, which were conducted by two or more Justices of the Peace. They dealt with petty theft, drunkenness, minor assaults, larceny, trespassing, bastardy, fraud and juvenile cases, as well as ale licencing and adoption. There were some offences directly connected with the war. Those who sought to evade rationing and asociated price controls could be prosecuted. So could slackers in essential occupations. Petty Sessions registers provide formal records of proceedings. Minute books may be more detailed if they survive. They are likely to give dates, the names of defendants and complainants, details of offences, other details, and the judgement. There may be separate records for juvenile offences.

Quarter Sessions dealt with those offences which required trial by jury. A variety of records were kept. Order books and minute books are likely to record the basic details of cases. In some courts, recorders kept rough notebooks giving fuller (but sometimes unreadable) particulars. Sessions rolls include case papers, which may include indictments (formal charges), depositions (the statements of witnesses) and other papers. These may also be filed separately. There may be registers of convictions, and calendars of prisoners.

Calendars of prisoners tried at Quarter Sessions can also be found in TNA HO140 (which also includes calendars of prisoners tried at Assizes). These calendars give the names, ages, and trades of prisoners, together with the dates of the warrant, the arrest, and the trial. Charges are noted, together with the names of victims. Finally, the verdict of the jury, and the sentence of the court, are stated. These calendars are arranged chronologically and alphabetically by county.

Both petty and quarter sessions also dealt with some non-criminal business, for example, bastardy and licencing. Bastardy records are discussed by Ruth Paley in her *My ancestor was a bastard* (Rev reprint. Society of Genealogist Enterprises, 2011). For licencing records, see Jeremy Gibson's *Victuallers' licences: records for family and local historians* (3rd ed. Family History Partnership, 2009). Quarter sessions also dealt with adoptions, for which there are separate registers. For a detailed listing of Quarter Sessions records, consult:

♦ GIBSON, JEREMY. *Quarter Sessions records for family historians: a select list.* 5th ed. Family History Partnership, 2007.

Some of the more serious offences, such as those subject to capital punishment, were sent to the Assize courts. The records of these courts are in TNA, in the ASSI series. There may also be references to the Assizes amongst Quarter Session records (and see the calendars of prisoners in TNA, HO140 as noted above). A key to Assize records is provided at **www.nationalarchives. gov.uk/records/research-guides/assizes-key-criminal-1559-1971.htm** (for Wales, **www.nationalarchives.gov.uk/records/research-guides/assizes-key-welsh-1831-1971.htm**).

Assize cases are listed in the Crown minute, gaol and agenda books, which summarise cases heard or to be heard, and frequently note the plea, the verdict, and the sentence. Indictment files are also available. Indictments were written on printed forms, and give the name, the residence, and the occupation of the defendant (although these details may be fraudulent). They also indicate the statute which had been infringed. Indictments are usually annotated with notes of the plea, the verdict, and the sentence; the names of prosecution witnesses may also be given. Indictment files may also include recognizances, gaol calendars, coroners' inquisitions, examinations and depositions, and related documents. Depositions – witness statements, and case papers - may also be available in separate files. These can be searched for by the accused's name on TNA's online discovery catalogue **http://discovery.nationalarchives.gov.uk**.

For a more detailed overview of Assize records, visit:
♦ Criminal trials in the assize courts 1559-1971
  www.nationalarchives.gov.uk/records/research-guides/
    assizes-criminal-1559-1971.htm

In the Metropolis, a different system operated. The Central Criminal Court (popularly known as the Old Bailey) was empowered to try treasons, murders, felonies, and misdemeanors; it had jurisdiction over London, Middlesex and parts of Essex, Kent, and Surrey, as well as on the high seas and abroad. Its records are in TNA. Registers of prosecutions undertaken by the Director of Public Prosecutions are in DPP9. Depositions are in CRIM1, with an index to those sent up from magistrates and coroners courts in CRIM2. Indictments – the formal statement of the charge – are in CRIM4, indexed in CRIM5. They are generally endorsed with the plea of the accused, and the jury's verdict. These files may also include subsidiary documents, such as coroner's inquisitions, gaol deliveries, and recognizances. The Court Books in CRIM6 are brief records of cases heard, noting the plea, the verdict, and the sentence. They are arranged in chronological order, but un-indexed.

Appeals were heard by the Court of Criminal Appeal, whose registers (in J81) give appellants' names, details of the conviction, the nature of the appeal, and its outcome. They are not indexed. For more details, see:
♦ Serious crimes: trials in the Old Bailey and the Central Criminal Court
  www.nationalarchives.gov.uk/records/research-guides/old-bailey.htm

Prisons were the responsibility of the Prison Commissioners, whose records are in TNA. Class PCOM2 includes registers of prisoners and habitual criminals, photograph albums, minute books, visitors' books, order books, journals, assizes and quarter sessions calendars and other records. There are some personal files on prisoners convicted of murder in PCOM9, although these may still be closed. Records of individual prisons may have been deposited locally.

Under the Prevention of Crime Act 1869, registers of habitual criminals were ordered to be kept. By 1939, these were the responsibility of the Criminal Record

Office, and are now in TNA, class MEPO6. They should list everyone sent to prison for a term of one month or more. Information from these registers was published in the *Police Gazette*, which is also held in this class. The latter had six supplements, all of which may provide useful information. Various supplements provided details of active travelling criminals, convicts on licence and persons under police supervision, wanted for offences, absentees and deserters from HM Forces, and photographs of active criminal. Deaths of criminals were recorded in another supplement. These are all in MEPO6, but are also held by the Open University **http://www8.open.ac.uk/library/library-resources/the-open-university-archive/police-collections,** where fuller details are given. Some issues may be found amongst the archives of local police forces. There may be restrictions on access.

Young offenders can be traced in the registers of the institutions to which they were sent. Some of these were run by the Borstal Association, whose registers and case files are in HO247 – although closed for 75 years. The records of approved schools are frequently lodged with local record offices; London Metropolitan Archives, for example, has various registers, including a file on the evacuation of approved schools and remand homes.

14. Internees and Conscientious Objectors

There were many Germans and Italians in the UK in 1939. There were also many supporters of the British Union of Fascists, led by Oswald Mosley. They were all considered to be a threat to British security – potential spies, or Nazi sympathisers. Conscientious objectors were also seen as a problem by the authorities, although there was some sympathy for them.

In September 1939, MI5 wanted to detain all the c.60,000-75,000 Germans and Austrians in the country. Many, of course, were refugees, and the Home Office trimmed the list drastically. Four months after the commencement of the war, only 554 were in detention. Another 6,500 had restrictions placed on their movement. All the rest had to register with the police – a requirement which all had to meet anyway. Subsequently, the net widened considerably. Thousands were rounded up at the time of the Dunkirk crisis. Many Italians were detained when Italy declared war. Numerous aliens spent the war in a camp on the Isle of Man. Others were sent to the colonies, although this policy was stopped after ships carrying them were sunk by U-boats. As the war progressed, it was realised that the majority of the internees were not in fact a threat; ironically, many were Jews. By the end of the war, most had been either released or repatriated.

Records of some 200,000 individual internees can be found in TNA, class HO396. These index cards record the names, dates of birth, nationality, police registration numbers, UK addresses, occupations, and details of employers, together with decisions of the tribunals which decided on internment. Digitised images of the fronts of these cards are available on TNA's Digital Microfilm page **www.nationalarchives.gov.uk/documentsonline/digital-microfilm.asp.** Files from this class listing 'internees at liberty in the UK' are also available at Moving Here **www.movinghere.org.uk**. The records are mostly arranged by nationality, with separate files for those shipped out to Canada or Australia, those released, and various other categories. Individual internees may be recorded in several different files. If a tribunal decided that a person should be interned, details of the case are noted on the back of these cards. The backs of cards have not been digitised, and appear to be still closed to public inspection. Internees sent to the colonies can be traced in the passenger lists of the Board of Trade, which can be searched at Ancestors on Board **www.ancestorsonboard.com**. Some other files can be found in TNA, class HO 215.

The requirement on aliens to register with the police also left records. Where these have survived, they are likely to be in local record offices, which may also hold files from local Aliens Tribunals. West Sussex Record Office, for example, has a schedule of aliens who appeared before the local Aliens Tribunal (POL/W/HQ/15/6). Selected aliens registration cards from the Metropolitan Police can be found in TNA, class MEPO 35. These are also available on TNA's Digital Microfilm page. Aliens who applied for naturalisation are listed in TNA class HO 405. Some personal files on aliens are in HO382. Other records of aliens and internees in local record offices are listed by Roger Kershaw and Mark Pearsall in their *Immigrants and aliens: a guide to sources on UK immigration and citizenship* (Readers Guide 25. The National Archives, 2004).

For a select bibliography of 'Internment During World Wars I & II', which includes some manuscript material held by the Manx Museum, visit: **www.gov.im/mnh/heritage/library/bibliographies/internment.xml**

In addition to aliens, many British subjects were also detained under the Defence of the Realm regulation 18B. Some were pacifists, but the great majority were members of the British Union of Fascists – including their leader, Oswald Mosley – or otherwise sympathetic to Nazi ideology. Many personal files for them can be found scattered throughout Home Office and KV (MI5) files in

TNA. Details can be found by searching TNA's catalogue by name. Many can also be found by searching words such as 'detained', 'interned', or 'regulation 18B'. Personal files on those whom MI5 took an interest in can be found in TNA, class KV2. I understand that there is a 1939 list of members of the British Union of Fascists in TNA, HO45/25754.

Some pacifists were detained in company with the Fascists, but most conscientious objectors who could convince authority of their beliefs were directed into non-combatant roles. Even before the war began, they could register with the Ministry of Labour and National Service. They had to appear before one of 17 regional tribunals. About 59,000 registered, but c.12,000 failed to prove their case and were not exempted from the call-up. Some of the latter refused to serve, and were imprisoned. Most of those exempted from service were directed into agriculture or civil defence work, although some were conscripted into non-combatant roles in the Army.

Records of tribunals can sometimes be found in local record offices. A nominal register of some conscientious objectors is in TNA class LAB45/75-6 & 84. Other sample documents relating to particular individuals are in LAB45/51-60. Many other papers on the subject are held by TNA; these are mostly related to policy rather than individuals. Some personal papers of conscientious objectors are held by the Peace Pledge Union archives **www.pret.org.uk.**.

A detailed history of wartime internment, mentioning many names, is provided by:

♦ SIMPSON, A.W. BRIAN. *In the highest degree odious: detention without trial in wartime Britain.* Oxford University Press, 1992.

The camp on the Isle of Man is the subject of:

♦ CHAPPELL, CONNERY. *Island of barbed wire: internment on the Isle of Man in World War Two.* Robert Hale, 2005.

For conscientious objectors, see:

♦ BARKER, RACHEL. *Conscience, government, and war: conscientious objection in Great Britain, 1939-45.* Routledge & Kegan Paul, 1982.

See also the CO Project webpage:

♦ CO Project: archive & educational resource **www.ppu.org.uk/coproject**

15. Voluntary Organizations

A variety of voluntary organizations were active during the War. Many records relating to them are available, and are described below. Two of them – the British Red Cross, and the St John Ambulance - have cooperated to produce an interesting website on their joint activities during war-time:

♦ Caring on the Home Front - Volunteer memories from World War Two
   www.caringonthehomefront.org.uk

Friends Ambulance Unit
This was a volunteer ambulance service, established by Quakers, and run mainly by conscientious objectors. Its extensive archives are in Friends House Library **www.quaker.org.uk/library**.

Red Cross
The Red Cross was founded to provide medical aid to the sick and wounded in time of war, but expanded its work to help civilians in peace-time as well. During the war, its volunteers were heavily involved in the Blitz, and cooperated closely with the emergency services and civil defence. Its museum holds an index of personnel who served during the war, together with a variety of relevant books and archives. For details of holdings, and for various 'historical factsheets' concerning its war-time activities, visit:

♦ British Red Cross: Museum and Archives
   www.redcross.org.uk/About-us/Who-we-are/Museum-and-archives

St Johns Ambulance Brigade
This was another voluntary medical service, operated by the Order of St John of Jerusalem. For details of resources for researching its volunteers, visit:

♦ St John Ambulance: The Library: researching: St John Ambulance history
   www.sja.org.uk/sja/about-us/our-library/researching-sja.aspx

Salvation Army
The Salvation Army was established by 'General' William Booth in the late nineteenth century as an evangelical Christian organization which set out to meet the social needs of those it sought to evangelize, and to fight for social justice. During the war its mobile canteens were welcomed in bombed out areas, and in air raid

shelters. Its clothing stores were valued by those who lost all their clothing in the Blitz. It ran Red Shield clubs and station canteens for the armed forces, and even a hotel for Canadian servicemen in London. The status of its personnel is described in military terms: 'soldiers' are ordinary members, recorded in registers kept at local corps headquarters. The records of officers, that is, full-time workers, are kept at the Army's Territorial Headquarters. Many records were lost during the war, but some have survived. It may not always be possible to see surviving records, but information from them may be available. The Salvation Army also published a variety of journals (listed by Wiggins – see below), which include much personal information. Runs of many of these journals, together with surviving archives, of the Army's central administration, are held at:

♦ Salvation Army: International Heritage Centre
   www.salvationarmy.org.uk/uki/heritage

For a detailed guide to Salvation Army records, see:
♦ WIGGINS, RAY. *My ancestors were in the* Salvation Army*: how can I find out more about them?* 2nd ed. Society of Genealogists, 1999.

Women's Voluntary Service

The WVS was founded in 1938 as the Women's Voluntary Service for Air Raid Precautions. It was formed to assist civilians during and after air raids, and provided emergency rest centres, canteens, first aid, and assistance with the evacuation and billeting of children. By 1943, it had over 1,000,000 volunteers, and had expanded its activities to cover just about every aspect of wartime life, from knitting to the collection of salvage. At its height, there were almost 2,000 centres throughout the country, and its history (with a booklist) is briefly recounted on its website **www.wrvs.org.uk/about-us/our-history.** Its activites were sometimes reported in newspapers, which are worth checking (see chater 7).

The work of the WVS continues to this day, although its role has changed. Its 40,000 volunteers now provide a wide range of services, especially for older people, e.g. meals on wheels. The name changed to the Womens Royal Voluntary Service in 1966.

The WRVS Archive and Heritage Collection **www.wrvs.org.uk/about-us/our-history/wrvs-archive-and-heritage-collection** has some 2,000,000 documents, plus 15,000 photographs, related to WRVS activities from its beginnings up to the present day. The narrative reports, compiled (originally monthly) for each centre, form a major proportion of this archive, and provide a great deal of information concerning its war-time and subsequent activities. The names of members killed during the war are listed on its Roll of Honour **www.wrvs.org. uk/Uploads/Documents/About%20us/roll_of_honour.pdf,** with details of how they died. Archives relating to the war-time local activities of the WVS have sometimes been deposited in local record offices.

Womens Institute

The Womens Institute (WI) was founded in 1915; it was (and is) a movement of rural women, giving them the opportunity to meet together, to have their say on the issues confronting them, and to be educated. Its meetings were (and are) important meeting places for rural women. During World War Two, the WI played a major role in assisting evacuees, in promoting British self-reliance in food, and in feeding the Home Guard and everyone else who needed feeding. There was a particularly close relationship between the Home Guard and the WI; after all, the husbands of many WI members were serving in the Home Guard.

WI records are held by London Metropolitan University's Womens Library, and are calendared on both A2A **www.nationalarchives.gov.uk/a2a** and Aim25 **www.aim25.ac.uk**. County federations and local branches have frequently deposited their minutes and other records in local record office; these sometimes include lists of members. For a brief account of WI history, see:

♦ The WI: History
   www.thewi.org.uk/standard.aspx?id=56

A full account is provided by:
♦ ROBINSON, JANE. *A force to be reckoned with: a history of the Women's Institute*. Virago Press, 2011.

Young Mens Christian Association

The YMCA was established as an evangelical Christian organization in 1844, but later flourished as a provider of social activities for its members. During the war, it established mobile canteens for the troops, and provided support for displaced people, refugees and prisoners of war. Its archive is held by the University of Birmingham. For details, consult:

♦ University of Birmingham Special Collections-research
   www.special-coll.bham.ac.uk/archives/guide.shtml

Young Womens Christian Association

The YWCA originated in much the same way as the YMCA, although it was a completely separate organization. During the war, it ran hostels for munitions workers and Land Army girls; it also provided rest rooms at railway stations, and mobile clubs. The archives of its central organization are held at the Modern Records Centre of Warwick University, and are described at:

♦ Modern Records Centre: Records of the Young Women's Christian Association (YWCA) 1855-1955

www2.warwick.ac.uk/services/library/mrc

(click 'archive search' and search 'Young Women's Christian Association')

16. Evacuation

The government was well aware of the threat of bombing to London and other major cities. Its response was to plan for evacuation. The problem was that relocating most of the activities carried out in London would probably be impossible, and that the nation could not continue if these activities were forced to cease by bombing. Nevertheless, some activities could be moved. All genealogists should be aware that the General Register Office was transferred to Llandudno for the duration of the war. Similar, the Ministry of Food went to South Wales. Other organizations were encouraged to move if they could. The London School of Economics spent the war in Cambridge. Lloyds of London leased Pinewood Film Studios at Iver in Buckinghamshire. The boys of Bristol's Clifton College spent the war in Bude, and those of Liverpool's Blue Coat School were sent to Beaumaris on Anglesey. However, plans for wholesale evacuation of government offices petered out when the move of 1300 Ministry of Labour staff to Southport attracted stinging criticism from the staff involved. Business enthusiasm for evacuation similarly waned.

Nevertheless, perhaps 2,000,000 people removed themselves from danger zones as war approached in 1939. The government's scheme made provision for expectant mothers, the frail elderly, the disabled, and the chonically sick. However, the major evacuation effort was directed at children. They were to be evacuated with their entire school communities. The first evacuation actually took place in the days immediately preceding the outbreak of war. However, not all of those who were eligible to be evacuated wanted to go. Of the 1,800,000 potential evacuees in London, only 660,000 actually went. They included 377,000 children with their teachers, 275,000 mothers and children, 3,500 expectant mothers, and a similar number of blind adults. In the provinces, only 1,200,000 out of a possible 3,600,000 went.

There was no compulsion – except for some billeters – and when no bombs fell on London in the first few weeks of war many children drifted back to the capital. There were later flurries of evacuation following the fall of France, at the onset of the Blitz in 1940, and when flying bombs began to fall in 1944.

Evacuation was administered by local authorities, under the direction of the Ministry of Health. The Ministry of Education was also heavily involved, Many papers relating to evacuation survive in both TNA, and amongst the records of local authorities. However, the majority of these archives relate to policy and administration, rather than to individual evacuees. Catalogue descriptions frequently give little indication of how useful files might be for tracing people.

There was no central register of evacuees. Those eligible to take part had to register; the registers may survive amongst school records. When they arrived at their destinations, they had to be billeted. Local authorities were expected to arrange billeting. In Hastings, registers of evacuees (now in East Sussex Record Office, reference dhba/DH/B/1) were compiled giving names of householders, names of evacuees, dates of billeting, and notes of removals to new addresses. They record weekly payments made to those receiving evacuees, with the payable for accompanied and unaccompanied children, adults, expectant mothers, blind persons, teachers and helpers. Similar registers are frequently available in the evacuation areas.

The children also had to be educated. School admittance and attendance registers therefore constitute one of the major sources for tracing evacuees. These are considered in the next chapter.

Another possible source of information are the memoirs of the evacuees themselves. These can frequently be found in record offices and libraries, both printed, manuscript, and indeed, sound. The Imperial War Museum **www.iwm.org.uk** has a good collection of such material. The Museum of London **www.museum oflondon.org.uk**, and the British Library National Sound Archive **www.bl.uk/nsa**, both have good oral history collections. Similar material is held by the Second World War Experience Centre **www.war-experience. org/research/default.asp**.

Some children were sent overseas. In 1940, over 2600 were evacuated to Canada, Australia, New Zealand, and South Africa, under the auspices of the Childrens Overseas Reception Board (CORB). This Board had been established in response to offers of hospitality made by the governments of these countries. They followed almost 14,000 who had been sent out be private charities immediately before the outbreak of war.

Child history cards, now held in TNA, class DO131/106-13, record the childrens' names, dates of birth, places of residence, details of parents, details of their placements abroad, and notes on their health, schooling, and employment. They are fully searchable on TNA's catalogue. Briefer details can also be found on the Board of Trade's passenger lists in BT 27, which can be searched at Ancestors Onboard **www.ancestorsonboard.com**. The programme ceased when SS Benares was sunk by a German U-boat in mid-Atlantic, with the loss of 134 passengers, including 70 CORB children.

There are numerous books on war-time evacuation. A good general account, with a useful bibliographic overview, is provided by:

♦ WELSHMAN, JOHN. *Churchill's children : the evacuee experience in wartime Britain*. Oxford University Press, 2010.

There is a greater emphasis on overseas evacuation in:

♦ JACKSON, CARLTON. *Who will take our children?* Methuen, 1985.

For evacuation from London, see the London Metropolitan Archives information leaflet on:

♦ The evacuation of Children from the County of London during the Second World War 1939-1945

www.cityoflondon.gov.uk/Corporation/LGNL_Services/Leisure_and_ culture/Records_and_archives/Visitor_information/free_information_ leaflets.htm (click title)

For children sent overseas, see:

♦ MANN, JESSICA. *Out of harm's way : the wartime evacuation of children from Britain*. Headline, 2005.

Child migration in World War II is set in its longer context by:

KERSHAW, ROGER, & SACKS, JANET. *New lives for old: the story of Britain's*
♦ *child migrants*. National Archives, 2008.

17. Education

In 1939, schooling up to the age of 14 was compulsory. Elementary schools catered for children up to age 11; older children were taught in secondary schools run by local councils. The Church of England, other christian denominations, and a variety of charitable organizations, also ran many schools. There were also fee-paying public schools, such as Eton, for the elite.

The Second World War severely disrupted children's education at all levels. It has already been seen how many schools were forced to evacuate from the major urban centres to the countryside. In 1939, entire schools were evacuated. The many children whose parents refused to let them go were frequently left without a school to attend. Sometimes, the evacuees themselves could only be taught part-time, as they had to share resources with the schools in the evacuation areas. At times during the war, up to a million children were without schools.

Some of the evacuated schools continued to operate independently; for example, North London's Jewish Girls Secondary School was based in Shefford, Essex, for the whole of the war. Its headmistress, Judith Grunfeld, recounted its experiences in her *Shefford: The Study of a Jewish School Community in Evacuation 1939-1945* (Essex, 1980). Sometimes, schools temporarily lost their separate identity, and were merged with schools in the evacuation areas.

The names of both local children, and evacuees, can be found in school registers and log books, which are frequently beld by local record offices. Devon Record Office, for example, has a 'register of admission, progress and withdrawal' for Brendon Parochial School (637C/EFA 1). There are also evacuees' attendance registers, together with other papers concerning evacuees. A school log-book records life at the school. In the back of the admission register for Teignmouth Secondary School (also in Devon Record Office, 3244 C/2) are loose papers which give the names of evacuees, together with both their local and home addresses. Accounts of the evacuation may also sometimes be found in the school magazines of those schools which were affected.

For the public schools of the elite, many registers have been published. A good collection of these is held by the Society of Genealogists, and is listed in:

♦ *School, university and college registers and histories in the library of the Society of Genealogists.* 2nd ed. Society of Genealogists, 1996.

The war-time experiences of many individual public schools"schools is described in:

♦ *Schools at war: a story of education, evacuation and endurance in the Second World War.* Phillimore, 2005.

Teachers can also be identified from school records. They had to register with the Teachers Registration Council. Its records have been digitised, and can be searched at:

♦ Teachers Registration Council Registers 1914-1948
 www.findmypast.co.uk/search/teachers-registrations

18. Occupational Sources

Unemployment was virtually absent from war-time Britain. Everybody had a job, except for the young, the disabled, and the elderly. The manpower demands of the armed forces were heavy. In May 1939, the Military Training Act made all males aged between 20 and 22 liable to be called up for 6 months military training. On the outbreak of war, conscription was extended to most males aged between 18 and 40. In 1941, the age limit was raised to 51. In the same year, women in their twenties were also conscripted, although they were required to undertake essential war work, rather than combat duties. Many served in the Womens Land Army, or in munitions factories.

Conscription into the armed forces was vital to the war effort – but so was agriculture, mining, transport, the merchant navy, some manufacturing (especially munitions), and a range of other industries. In the First World War, many men who worked in some of these industries had been conscripted – and much needed production had slumped. The government in 1939 was not going to make the same mistake again. Men working in essential industries were exempted from military service from the outset of the war. If a man did not serve in the armed forces, it is quite likely that he was in one of these occupations.

Food production in a London square.

Conscientious objectors were frequently conscripted into these 'reserved occupations'.

Many sources relating to these and other occupations are available. For an introductory survey of occupational sources, see my *Trades and professions: the family historian's guide* (Family History Partnership, 2011). Numerous books and journal articles on particular occupations are available; they are listed in my *Occupational sources for genealogists* (2nd ed. Federation of Family History Societies, 1996), and in the county volumes of my *British genealogical library guides* series. The latter includes separate volumes on *Londoners occupations: a genealogical guide* (2nd ed. 2001), *Surrey and Sussex occupations: a genealogical guide* (2001), and *Yorkshire occupations: a genealogical guide* (2000).

A variety of general sources for occupational information are available; some have already been mentioned. Trade directories are likely to record professionals, tradesmen, and farmers. Governmental regulation of particular occupations, such as innkeepers, teachers, and the medical professions, led to extensive records being kept. Professional organizations and trade unions kept records of their membership, and sometimes issued journals or newsletters which contain information about them. Employers maintained personnel records, frequently including information about staff called up. For example, Bedfordshire & Luton Archive Service hold a number of files (Li PM) on wartime staffing of the county library service, including a file regarding the call-up of female library staff for National Service, and a full list of staff members. Sources for those occupations which made important contributions to the war effort are our primary concern here.

Civil Servants

The war could not have been fought without the Civil Service. Some ministries, such as the Ministry of Defence, were more directly concerned with the war effort than others. However, even the work of the Ministry of Agriculture was essential: without it, those who stayed at home might not have been fed.

There is no one source for identifying civil servants, apart from the listings of examination marks in TNA, class CSC 10. Examination was the only route into the Civil Service. Most application papers have been destroyed; a few relating to famous individuals can be found in CSC11. Personal files of senior officers can sometimes be found amongst departmental establishment files; for example, files for Treasury officials can be found in T268; Ministry of Health personal files can be found in MH107; Ministry of Food files are in MAF128. The Treasury was sometimes involved in the recruitment of staff to other departments; there are records in T161 and T162.

Many other records may perhaps be found by consulting the establishment files of the relevant departments, although it is generally unlikely that personal files will be found. A time consuming search may, however, locate staff lists and files relating to promotions, staff moves, etc. Such papers can sometimes be traced through TNA's catalogue.

War memorials and rolls of honour were prepared for many departments; for example, Air Ministry staff are recorded by AIR 2/13661. Prison service staff who lost their lives or were awarded decorations are memorialised in PCOM 9/2213. For information on the construction of a war memorial for Colonial Office staff, see CO 866/58/5. A file on the office war memorial for the Commissioners of Crown Lands is held at CRES3/49.

Departments frequently compiled files concerning staff serving with the armed forces. Ministry of Agriculture staff honours and casualty lists are in

MAF39/149. Ministry of Health staff from the training ship 'Cornwall' who were on active service can be identified in MH 102/242. Many similar files can be found.

The records of civil service trade unions may be of help where they include membership records, or the journals and newsletters that they issued. Many are held by the Modern Records Centre at Warwick University **http://www2.warwick. ac.uk/services/library/mrc**. Journals such as the Inland Revenue Staff Federation's *Taxes* may provide valuable information about union members, and are sometimes more widely available in major research libraries.

For senior and some middle ranking civil servants, it is usually best to start by searching published sources. They were officially listed in the *British Imperial Calendar,* with details of their ranks; the sections in which they were working are also identified. Similar information may be found in *Whitakers Almanac.* The Colonial Office *List* and the Foreign Office *List* had more restricted remits, but are useful for the ministries they cover. If you consult several of these volumes in sequence, you should be able to trace a senior civil servant's career path. For officers of the Colonial Service, see A.H.M. Kirk-Greene's *Biographical Dictionary of the British Colonial Service 1939-1966* (H. Zall, 1991).

TNA's website includes a useful guide to:
♦ Civil Servants Personnel Records
   www.nationalarchives.gov.uk/records/research-guides/civil-servants.htm

Coalminers
At the outbreak of war, the government under-estimated the importance of the mining workforce, and conscripted many miners into the armed forces. Consequently, a severe shortage of miners developed. By mid-1943, 36,000 workers had disappeared, and the country's increasingly desperate need for coal forced the government to direct 10% of conscripts to the mines. They were chosen by ballot, and were known as the Bevin Boys, after Ernest Bevin, the wartime Minister of Labour and National Service. Some conscientious objectors were also recruited. They were not disbanded until 1948.

Most of the records of the Bevin Boys have been destroyed. TNA has a small collection of files (LAB45/94-8) containing names of individual ballotees, volunteers and optants from the Midlands Regional Office. Its other records relate to policy and procedures. For a brief description of these records, see:

♦ Your Archives: Bevin Boys
   http://yourarchives.nationalarchives.gov.uk/index.php?title=Bevin_Boys

The Bevin Boys Association **www.seniorsnetwork.co.uk/bevinboys/index.htm** is currently trying to trace all 48,000 Bevin Boys. Its archivist, Warwick Taylor, has recounted their history in his *The forgotten conscript: a history of the Bevin Boy* (2nd ed. Babash Ryan, 2003).

   The Bevin boys were trained by, and worked alongside, men who were life-long miners. A variety of sources are available for tracing coalminers; a comprehensive guide (including some additional information about the Bevin Boys, is provided by:

♦ TONKS, DAVID. *My ancestor was a coalminer*. [2nd ed.] Society of Genealogists Enterprises, 2010.

Deaths in the mines are listed by the National Database of Mining Deaths in Great Britain, which is hosted by:
♦ The Coal Mining History Resource Centre
   www.cmhrc.co.uk

Coastguards
HM Coastguard was a Board of Trade responsibility between 1922 and 1939. In 1939 responsibility was briefly transferred to the Ministry of Shipping, before the Admiralty took charge in 1940. During the war, the Coastguard took on the additional duty of war watch, and officers were armed.

   Few records of war-time coastguards are readily available. Officers are listed in the *Navy list*. Runs are available in major reference libraries, but the confidential print, issued for service use only, includes much more detail than the public version. Copies are held in TNA, class ADM177. Chief officers' service records are in TNA, class ADM 175/109-10; these records are digitised at **www.nationalarchives.gov.uk/documentsonline/digital-microfilm.asp**. This database also includes registers of deaths other than from enemy action (ADM104/13-17, with indexes in ADM104/106-7). Quarterly commendations lists are in BT166/3. For medals, consult BT 166/34-5.

Farmers
The production of food was vital to the war effort, and the farmers who produced it were exempted from conscription. They were not, however, exempt from

central direction of their efforts. The Ministry of Agriculture Fisheries & Food established county War Agricultural Executive Committees (frequently referred to as County War Ags). These had wide powers to increase production, including the ability to take possession of land being badly managed. They launched a ploughing up campaign to bring wide acres of grassland back into arable production. Their minutes, correspondence, and other papers, may sometimes provide information about particular farmers, although they may be tedious to search. They can be found in TNA, MAF80. Sometimes, related material can be found in local record offices.

The County War Ags had initially conducted a survey to inform their ploughing up campaign. Unfortunately, only a statistical summary (MAF38/213) survives from this survey; information of use to family historians is minimal. The returns from the National Farm Survey of 1941-3, which was conducted in order to provide information for post-war agricultural planning, are of much greater interest.

This survey covered all agricultural properties in England and Wales of five acres or more. If your ancestor farmed such a property, the likelihood is that useful information about him and his farm is available. The returns compiled by farmers, and the 'primary farm record' compiled by an inspector, are in TNA, class MAF32, arranged by county and parish. Maps compiled for the survey (which use Ordnance Survey maps as a base) are in MAF73.

The names of farmers in MAF32 are not separately indexed. It may therefore be helpful to check the relevant map first; it will show you where the farm was, and gives a unique code which will help you to find the individual returns in the collection for the parish (which may contain hundreds of documents).

The farmer had to complete three returns (although sometimes only two were sent in). The first recorded small fruit, vegetables, bulbs, flowers, and stocks of hay and straw. The second was a return of agricultural land, showing arable and pasture acreages, farm livestock, and statistical details of labour employed. A supplementary return asked further questions concerning labour, motive power (horses and tractors etc), and details of tenancies. The latter may be helpful, as it included a question on length of tenancy.

A further form was compiled by an inspector, based upon visiting the farm and observing. This was the primary farm record, and had four sections: tenure, conditions of farm, water and electricity, and management. The latter may be particularly helpful as it attempts a classification of managerial practice. The best farmers were rated A, those who were up to the task rated B, but poor managers were rated C. The reasons for a B or C rating had to be given; they might include old age, lack of capital, or personal failings. If the latter, the inspector had to provide an explanation, and might make personal comments on the farmer himself. There was also space for the inspector to write other comments.

These forms provide much useful information. They directly link farmers to the land they farmed, and give details of tenancies (including the names of landowners). If they were elderly, or widows/widowers, this might be noted. Smallholders frequently also worked in other rural occupations, such as thatchers, wheelwrights, or millers. If they were close to a town, they might combine farming with more urban occupations. Many smallholders, in both town and country, were also innkeepers. Such dual occupations were recorded. Occupations of the husbands of married women who were farming on their own account might be noted. The supplementary form provided space to record the numbers of close relatives who worked on the farm; the information requested was statistical, but occasionally names might be given. Farming was frequently a family affair, so sons might be found farming their fathers' property; husbands in charge of their wives' farms.

A range of other personal information might also be provided, although, sadly, agricultural labourers are rarely mentioned by name. It is worth checking the forms for other farms in the parish; family members sometimes farmed properties close to each other.

For an online guide to these records, see:
♦ National Farm Surveys of England and Wales 1940-1943
   www.nationalarchives.gov.uk/records/research-guides/farm-survey.htm

More extensive information is provided by:
♦ BEECH, GERALDINE, & MITCHELL, ROSE. *Maps for family and local history: the records of the Tithe, Valuation Office and National Farm Surveys.* 2nd ed. National Archives, 2004.

For the general background to the survey, see:
♦ SHORT, BRIAN, WATKINS, CHARLES, FOOT, WILLIAM, & KINSMAN, PHIL. *The National Farm Survey 1941-1943: state surveillance and the countryside in England and Wales in the Second World War.* CABI Publishing, 1999.

Firemen
When war broke out, fire services were provided by about 1600 local authority fire brigades. In 1938, their work was augmented by the Auxiliary Fire Service,

which was founded to assist Civil Defence air raid precautions. Following the outbreak of war, the fire services needed to work together, but there was frequently confusion over who was in overall charge. The equipment used by different brigades was frequently incompatible, and each brigade had different rules and regulations. Consequently, in 1941 all the brigades were merged into one organization, the National Fire Service (NFS). A seperate National Fire Service (Northern Ireland) was created in 1942. At its peak, the NFS had 37,000 staff, including 70,000 women. Many files concerning the NFS are held by TNA, mainly in HO186 and HO187. These, however, are primarily concerned with policy and administration, rather than individual personnel.

After the war, responsibility for fire precautions reverted to counties and county boroughs, and the NFS was disbanded in 1947. Unfortunately, its personnel files would probably have been passed to the local fire brigades and may have subsequently been destroyed. It is, however, worth checking with your local record office. Bedfordshire and Luton Archives, for example, have personnel record cards from the local fire brigade which provide a great deal of information on wartime firemen. The London Fire Brigade Museum **www.london-fire.gov.uk/Research.asp** has an extensive research library, and may be able to help you trace NFS members from London – although there may be some restrictions on access to personal information.

Many firemen won gallantry awards during the war. A register of all awards made is in TNA, class HO187/1838. Firemen were eligible for the award of the Kings Police Medal, the name of which was changed to the Kings Police and Fire Services Medal in 1940 to reflect the eligibility of firemen. For details, see below p 52.

The Firefighters Memorial Trust **www.firefightersmemorial.co.uk** maintains a memorial to firemen who gave their lives in World War II; the names of those who gave their lives at other dates are also included. Its website includes a list of those remembered. A monument recording the names of London firefighters who lost their lives stands in Sermon Lane, near St Pauls Cathedral.

Lighthouse Keepers

The lights on many lighthouses were extinguished during the Second World War, but not all were extinguished outright. Some were merely dimmed, in order to aid navigation for the nation's shipping. There was plenty of work for lighthouse keepers, who were employed by Trinity House. Its records are held in Guildhall Library, and include a register of staff appointments, 1914-72, a 'station book', listing keepers and crews from 1941 to 1955, and registers of pensionable staff (for staff born before 1931). A variety of other records may also be relevant; for a detailed listing of this archive, see the Library's 'leaflet guide':

♦ Corporation of Trinity House: Family History Sources at Guildhall Library **www.history.ac.uk/gh/thouse2.htm**

Those lighthouse keepers who lost their lives during the war are commemorated on a memorial in Trinity Square, London.

Medical Professions

Medical staff were in great demand during the war, and many joined the armed forces. Doctors, nurses, and dentists had to be registered. The *Medical Register* lists doctors. It was (and is) published annually by the General Medical Council, and is arranged alphabetically by surname. It gives full names, addresses, the date of registration with the GMC, and details of qualifications obtained. The volumes for 1939, 1943 and 1947 can be searched on Ancestry at UK Medical Registers **www.ancestry.co.uk/doctors_records**. Issues for 1940 and 1943 can be searched at **www.familyrelatives.com**, which also offers the 1934 edition of the *Medical Directory.* Both the *Medical Register,* and the *Medical Directory,* are still published regularly. Runs can be found in major research libraries as well as online.

For nurses, it is necessary to consult the *Register of Nurses,* which was published annually during the war by the General Nursing Council. Registration became compulsory in 1943. The *Register* lists nurses by name (including maiden name where appropriate), registration date and place, address, and place and date of qualification. There are several sections in these volumes, and it may be necessary to search each section. The main section covers state registered nurses (SRNs), but there were also a number of different specialities, eg 'mental', and 'male'. Assistant nurses had lower qualifications, but were registered from 1943. The original registers for SRNs are available in TNA, class DT10. The roll of assistant nurses is in DT11. There are also lists of candidates for SRN examinations in DT27 and DT28.

Midwives were registered seperately; the Midwives roll in TNA, class DV7, was compiled on receipt of notifications by certified midwives of their intention to practice. Copies are held by a number of other institutions. Penal Board case files of the Central Midwives Board are in DV5, and can be searched by name in TNA's catalogue. The records of the Royal College of Midwives are now held with the archives of the Royal College of Obstetricians and Gynaecologists **www.rcog.org.uk/what-we-do/information-services/archives**.

Many nurses were trained by the Red Cross for service in the Voluntary Aid Detachments, which provided supplementary assistance to the Territorial Forces Medical Service. VAD nurses were not necessarily SRNs, or even 'Assistant Nurses'. They were trained in simple first aid and general nursing, but many performed clerical and kitchen duties, or took on roles such as ambulance drivers and welfare officers. Some worked overseas. Much of their work involved running auxiliary hospitals and convalescent homes in Britain.

The British Red Cross has extensive but incomplete series of index cards recording service details of VAD personnel. If a card can be found, it may include dates of service, the detachment(s) and institution(s) in which the nurse served, and details of any honours awarded. For further information, visit:

♦ War-time Volunteers and Personnel Records
  **www.redcross.org.uk/About-us/Who-we-are/Museum-and-archives/
  Resources-for-researchers/Volunteers-and-personnel-records**.

For more general information on tracing nurses, visit:
♦ Royal College of Nursing: genealogy and research advice
  **www.rcn.org.uk/development/rcn_archives/
  research_advice_-_tracing_nurses**

Registers of dentists are held by the British Dental Association **www.bda.org** and the General Dental Council **www.gdc-uk.org**. The latter also holds applications for admittance to the register.

If your medical ancestor was employed by a hospital, it may also be worth consulting its personnel records. These are listed in the Hospital Records Database **www.nationalarchives.gov.uk/hospitalrecords**, although some of these records may be subject to a closure period. This database also lists patient records such as registers.

First aid posts were provided by local authorities. These dealt with minor injuries, freeing up hospitals to deal with the more serious cases, and were frequently staffed by volunteers. Records of their staffing may be available in local record offices; for example, Wiltshire & Swindon Archives hold Trowbridge enrolment cards of volunteers for first aid posts, cleansing units and stretcher bearers, c.1940 (G15/229/3).

Ambulance services were also a local authority responsibility, although voluntary organizations such as St John Ambulance and Friends Ambulance Unit also played an important role. Again, records of their staffing may be found in local record offices. For example, Bolton Archive and Local Studies Service has a file (ABZ/46/32) on the 'Approval of Appointments' in the Emergency Ambulance Services for 1939-1943.

There is a very wide range of other sources of potential value. For a good introduction to the records of the medical professions, see:

♦ HIGGS, MICHELLE. *Tracing your medical ancestors: a guide for family historians*. Pen & Sword, 2011.

Munitions Workers

The production of munitions was obviously vital for the war effort. There were three major Royal Ordnance Factories (ROFs) dating from the First World War; these were the Royal Arsenal, Woolwich, the Royal Gunpowder Factory at Waltham Abbey (Essex), and the Royal Small Arms Factory at Enfield (Middlesex). These were complemented by a variety of other factories further away from London, built during the 1930s. Government factories were run by the Ministry of Supply. Imperial Chemical Industries also owned a number of munitions factories, and acted as agents for the Ministry in running a number of others. A few other private companies similarly acted as agents. Many of these factories depended on women workers.

Surviving personnel records of munitions workers are now fragmentary. Some records may be in TNA, although a lengthy search might be required to find very little. Local record offices may have personnel records of local munitions factories. For an overall view of labour in the munitions industries, see:

♦ INMAN, PEGGY. *Labour in the munitions industries*. H.M.S.O., 1957.

An interesting Welsh study of munitions workers is provided by:

♦ WILLIAMS, MARI A. *A forgotten army : the female* munitions workers *of South Wales, 1939-1945* University of Wales Press, 2002.

Police

In war-time, much was demanded of the police. Routine policing had to continue, despite the difficulties caused by the call-up and the bombing. Additional duties included the enforcement of emergency legislation, air-raid precautions, billeting arrangements and the guarding of vulnerable points. Police could be called upon to provide first aid to air raid victims, to ensure the initial security of aircraft crash sites, to handle unexploded bombs and clear people from their vicinity, to ensure compliance with lighting regulations, to prevent looting after air-raids. Yet many police had been recruited to the military. In Somerset, for example, 100 officers enlisted in the first eighteen months of war. Additional manpower therefore had to be recruited. The volunteers of the Special Constabulary were already available; they were to be supplemented by the First Police Reserve, the Police War Reservists, and the Women's Auxiliary Police Corps. In consequence, police force numbers were much larger than they had been in peace-time.

A wide range of police personnel records can be found in local record offices, although much has been lost or destroyed. Attestation papers may include brief physical descriptions, age, place of birth, trade, date of appointment, postings, and date of leaving. Discipline books provide similar information. Personal files may be available. Some records relating to criminals (see chapter 13) may include incidental information on individual policemen. There are similar records for the Metropolitan Police, which are now in TNA. Attestation ledgers, registers of leavers, and pension records in MEPO4 and MEPO21 give brief details of Met officers. The attestation ledgers in MEPO4 have been digitised at:

♦ Your Archives: Metropolitan Police Records Project
   http://yourarchives.nationalarchives.gov.uk/index.php?title=
   Metropolitan_Police_Records_of_Service

For further details of Met records of service, visit:
♦ Police: London Metropolitan Police records of service
   www.nationalarchives.gov.uk/records/research-guides/
   metropolitan-police.htm

In addition, the City of London Police Records Office possesses registers listing every member of the force, and also has personal files on most officers. See:
♦ History of the Metropolitan Police: Records of Service
   www.met.police.uk/history/records.htm

Police orders include much information on personnel matters, including recruit-ment, promotions, transfers, awards, retirements, and dismissals. They can frequently be found in local record offices. Metropolitan Police orders are in TNA, class MEPO7. Some are also held by the Open University, visit **www8. open.ac.uk/library/library-resources/the-open-university-archive/police-collections**. A partial database of police orders is available:

◆ Metropolitan Police Orders Database
   www.policeorders.co.uk

TNA's class MEPO2-4 includes some 16,000 files, including personal files of senior and some women officers, as well as files on disciplinary offences, the bribery of police officers, and their murder. MEPO 3/2354, for example, concerns the conviction of Ivor Novello, the actor, with Dora Grace, a constable, for conspiring to commit offences against the Motor Vehicles (Restriction of Use) Order 1942. MEPO 4 files are available for free download from Documents Online Digital Microfilm site **www.nationalarchives.gov.uk/documentsonline/digital-microfilm.asp**

Details of a number of databases, including a listing of World War II casualties, can be found on the family history pages of:
◆ Friends of the Metropolitan Police Historical Collections
   www.fomphc.org.uk/viewpage.php?page_id=1

Policemen who lost their lives in World War II are included in the lists at:
◆ Police Roll of Honour Trust
   www.policememorial.org.uk/index.html

Policemen who performed acts of exceptional courage and skill, or exhibited conspicuous devotion to duty, were awarded the Kings Police Medal (known as the Kings Police and Fire Services Medal from 1940). Awards are published in the *London Gazette* **www.london-gazette.co.uk,** and in Police Orders. Recommendations for the award are in TNA, class HO45 (which also includes recommendations for the Albert Medal and the British Empire Medal). A register of Metropolitan officers considered for the award is also held by TNA, class MEPO22/2. Various awards for gallantry won by members of the Metropolitan Police are listed at:
◆ Metropolitan Police Gallantry Awards 1939 - 1945
   www.historybytheyard.co.uk/gallantry_list_1939-1945.htm

Many personal details, as well as photographs, are included in:
◆ FARMERY, J. PETER. Police *gallantry: the King's Police Medal, the King's Police and Fire Service Medal and the Queen's Police Medal for Gallantry, 1909-78: a record of the circumstances leading to the award of the* medals. North Manly, New South Wales: Periter & Associates, 1995.

For more detailed introductions to police research, see:

♦ SHEARMAN, ANTONY. *My ancestor was a policeman: how can I find out more about him?* Society of Genealogists, 2000.

♦ WADE, STEPHEN. *Tracing your police ancestors*. Pen & Sword, 2009.

Record office holdings of police records are listed by:

♦ Guide to the archives of the police forces of England and Wales / Ian Bridgeman & Clive Emsley
www.open.ac.uk/Arts/history/policing/police-archives-guide/index.html

For the British Transport Police, see:

♦ Police: Transport Police
**www.nationalarchives.gov.uk/records/research-guides/
transport-police.htm**

Postal Workers

For the Post Office, war meant serious staff shortages. A third of its employees joined up within a few weeks of the declaration of war. It also faced added demands on its services: mail for the troops, the distribution of ration cards and public information, the rapid expansion of the telegraph network in preparation for D-Day. Nevertheless, and despite the bombing of post offices, the mail was rarely delayed for more than 48 hours.

War-time postmen should be easy to trace. Post Office staff records have generally been preserved; they include, for example, pensions and gratuities records, appointment records and establishment books. These are deposited in the British Postal Museum and Archive **http://postalheritage.org.uk**. The Museum's website includes a page on 'How the Post Office Went to War', together with a variety of related pages. It also hosts the Royal Mail Group War Memorial database.

Railwaymen

Railways were vital to the war effort. They helped to evacuate 1,300,000 people from their homes when war broke out. 300,000 survivors of the Dunkirk debacle would not have got home (or to hospital) without them. And the preparations for D-Day involved 24,500 special trains moving 230,000 soldiers and 12,000 tons of their baggage. Railwaymen were a 'reserved occupation', that is, not liable to call-up. Nevertheless, 110,000 railwaymen were enlisted in the armed forces. To compensate, there were 105,000 women working on the railways by 1943, compared to 25,000 in 1939. Many of those railwaymen who stayed at home – probably well over 100,000 - enlisted in the Home Guard. And 140,000 railwaymen trained as air raid protection wardens.

A variety of sources can be used to trace railwaymen – personnel files, trade union records, company magazines, and a variety of other documents. If you know which company your ancestor worked for, it may be possible to trace the jobs he actually did, how he was recruited, his pay, his promotions, and where he lived.

At the time of the outbreak of war, there were four major railway companies: the Great Western Railway, the London, Midland & Scottish Railway, the London & North Eastern Railway, and the Southern Railway. The surviving archives of these companies are now in TNA; a few staff records are available as digitised images on its website. The Great Western Railway staff records (RAIL 264) in particular are extensive. These can be searched by name on TNA's catalogue **www.nationalarchives.gov.uk/search.** So can the returns of staff at the stations and depots of the London & North Eastern Railway as at 31st October 1939 (RAIL 397/1-2). Records for the London Midland and Scottish Railway, and for Southern Railway are disappointing; only a handful of files in RAIL 426 and RAIL 651 relate to the war years. For a full listing of TNA holdings of staff records, consult appendix 3 of David T. Hawkings book, *Railway ancestors: a guide to the staff records of the railway companies of England and Wales, 1822-1947* (2nd ed. History Press, 2008).

A variety of other railway staff records are listed in TNA's in-depth guide:
♦   Railways: staff records
     www.nationalarchives.gov.uk/records/research-guides/railway-staff.htm.

Some of these records are indexed in:
♦ UK Railway Employment Records, 1833-1963
     www.ancestry.co.uk

See also:
♦ *Railway staff database & railway company details*. CD. Railway Ancestors Family History Society, [20—?]

Not all railway archives are held at Kew. Railway staff registers from the North East and North Wales, held by Cheshire Archives, are indexed in:
♦ Cheshire Archives & Local Studies Railways Staff Database
     http://archives.cheshire.gov.uk/default.aspx?page=70

Railway staff magazines are another invaluable source of information. They contain much information concerning staff activities – details of appointments, promotions, transfers, retirements, etc. They frequently carry obituaries. Good collections are held in TNA (class ZPER), at the National Railway Museum in York **www.nrm.org.uk**, by the Railway Ancestors Family History Society, and by the British Library, amongst others. For a database listing 1400 names mentioned in the *Great Western Railway magazine* for the period 1938-March 1943, and another 1500 names from the *Southern Railway magazine* for the period to 1942, visit **Ancestry.co.uk.**. The Railway Ancestors Family History Society has issued a number of guides, including *Printed sources for railway staff details* (2000). For an overview of staff magazines, see:

♦ FOWLER, SIMON. 'Reading between the lines', *Ancestors* **73**, 2008, p.26-8.

Railwaymen can also be traced through the membership records of their trade unions. The major unions were the National Union of Railwaymen and the Associated Society of Locomotive Engineers and Firemen. Some records of both (but not many for the war years) are held by the Modern Records Centre of the University of Warwick; see its guide to:

♦ Railwaymen: Trade Union Records
   **www2.warwick.ac.uk/services/library/mrc/explorefurther/
   subject_guides/family_history/rail**

Some union branches have deposited records in local record offices. These can be traced through the National Register of Archives **www.nationalarchives.gov. uk/nra**.

If an ancestor was involved in a railway accident, you may find details amongst the Parliamentary papers, which are held by many research libraries. Accident reports have been compiled for the Board of Trade, and are published annually amongst these papers, under the title *Return of numbers of accidents on railways in Great Britain and Ireland*. Details of railway accidents can also be found in TNA class RAIL1053. Many accident reports are available at:

♦ Railways Archive
   www.railwaysarchive.co.uk/faq.php

See also detailed accounts at:
♦ List of Rail Accidents in the United Kingdom
   en.wikipedia.org/wiki/List_of_rail_accidents_in_the_United_Kingdom

Acts of gallantry by railwaymen are recorded in various files of the pre-nationalisation railway companies. Their files are now in the various RAIL classes in TNA. A file on awards to railwaymen for gallantry is in RAIL390/1208. Individual recommendations for awards, 1941-44, are in RAIL1172/2323. Related correspondence can be found in RAIL1172/2318-22. RAIL425/5 is concerned with honours and awards given to staff of the London Midland and Scottish Railway Company, 1941-7.

If you have railway ancestors, it may be useful to contact the Railway Ancestors Family History Society **www.railwayancestors.org.uk/index.html**, some of whose publications have already been mentioned. It publishes a useful journal, the contents of which are listed on its website.

Further Reading

There are two detailed guides to railway archives specifically intended for family historians:

◆ DRUMMOND, DI. *Tracing your railway ancestors: a guide for family historians*. Pen & Sword, 2011.

◆ HARDY, FRANK. *My ancestor was a railway worker.* Society of Genealogists, 2009.

A more comprehensive approach (not just family history oriented) is taken by:

◆ EDWARDS, CLIFF. *Railway records: a guide to sources.* Public Record Office, 2001.

Most records relating to railwaymen during the Second World War are held by TNA. There are two in-depth guides on its website, both of which should be consulted:

◆ Railways: an Overview
  www.nationalarchives.gov.uk/records/research-guides/
  railway-overview.htm

Women's Land Army

It has already been noted that the country needed to be able to feed itself, and that conscription meant a drastic reduction in the agricultural labour force. The gap, as in other sectors, was filled by women. The Women's Land Army was established in June 1939. By September, over 1,000 women had volunteered for service. In 1941 there were 20,000 members, and at its peak in 1943 over 80,000

Land girls in action.

women had joined. The Timber Corps formed part of the organization; it had 6,000 members at its peak.

Sadly, the original service records do not seem to have survived. However, the index cards to them are available on 808 microfiche at TNA, class MAF421. These cards, dating from 1939-48, provide a limited amount of information on the individual's service – generally name, age, address when enlisted, and civilian occupation, although there could be other miscellaneous brief notes. The final sheet is a compilation of mis-sorts. For Scotland, similar index cards are held by the National Archives of Scotland.

Many records are in local repositories. For example, Staffordshire Record Office has lists of volunteers, together with details of committee members and farmers, at DL1002/2. For a brief general guide to sources, see:

♦ National Archives: Looking for records of the Women's Land Army
   www.nationalarchives.gov.uk/records/looking-for-person/
   womenslandarmy.htm?WT.lp=rg-3157

Many illustrations of land girl activities can be found by searching army' 1939-1945 at:

♦ Imperial War Museum Collections and Research
   www.cabinetwarrooms.org.uk/collections-research

For a tribute to the women of the Land Army, see:

♦ Womens Land Army Tribute
   www.womenslandarmytribute.co.uk/

The history of the Land Army is recounted in:

♦ TYRER, NICHOLA. *They fought in the fields: The Women's Land Army: the story of a forgotten army.* Tempus, 2007. Originally published 1996.

19. Further Reading

There is an enormous amount of literature on the history of the Second World War, which cannot even be summarised here. A bibliography of books on the war is provided by:

♦ ENSER, A.G.S. *A subject bibliography of the Second World War: books in English 1939-1974.* Deutsch, 1977.

♦ ENSER, A.G.S. *A subject bibliography of the Second World War, and after math: books in English 1975-1987.* 2nd ed. Gower, 1990.

For a useful guide to sources for ancestors who fought, which includes several chapters on the Home Front, see:

♦ TOMASELLI, PHIL. *Tracing your second world war ancestors: a guide for family historians.* Pen & Sword, 2011.

For an overall view of holdings relating to the war in TNA (formerly the Public Record Office), see:

♦ CANTWELL, JOHN. *The Second World War: a guide to documents in the Public Record Office.* 3rd ed. PRO Handbook 15. Rev. ed. Public Record Office, 1998.

though much has been written on the Home Front, there has been little previous attempt to survey the available sources. The principal exception to that rule is restricted to resources for London, and is primarily concerned with local rather than family history. However, many of the sources it discusses are of relevance to the family historian, and may be replicated elsewhere. An extensive bibliography of primary and secondary works is included in:

♦ CREATON, HEATHER. *Sources for the history of London 1939-45: a guide and bibliography*. Archives and the use series **9**. British Records Association, 1998.

Subject index